THE DARK MOON LILITH IN ASTROLOGY

*

Including her Ephemeris

*

By Ivy M. Goldstein-Jacobson

*

Member of

AMERICAN FEDERATION OF ASTROLOGERS
and
FIRST TEMPLE OF ASTROLOGY
at Los Angeles

Engravings by Marge J. Zander

Author of

Mathematics of the Astrological Chart
Here and There in Astrology
Foundation of the Astrological Chart
Simplified Horary Astrology
All Over the Earth Astrologically
The Turn of a Lifetime Astrologically
The Way of Astrology
Correspondence Course in Astrology

Photographed from Mrs. Jacobson's typing
and
Printed in the United States
by
Frank Severy Publishing
Alhambra, California

Affectionately dedicated to

my students and colleagues

in Astrology

Table of Contents

THE DARK MOON LILITH

There has been much mystery surrounding Lilith, the dark moon of the earth, and this is consistent because she represents that which is mysterious or obscure and hard to understand in human nature and especially in human frailty. She is a dark satellite, not luminous to us like the Moon; an enigma, her reason-for-being a mystery also, and difficult to distinguish in the darkness of life, so to say. She moves like a wraith that beckons us to follow, but if we do we live to regret it, for she appeals to that which lures mankind to his doom, his lower self, because she appears when he is vulnerable. Her symbol is ∅, a lesser moon diagonally divided.

Lilith was first observed around 1720. She is now noted at intervals of approximately six months but only by her shadow as she crosses the face of the Sun. Her cycle is 126 years and her daily motion, always direct, is 3 degrees, 2 minutes. Her ephemeris herein (p. 27) gives her position on the first of each month. To find her place on another date, take the difference-in-days and multiply it separately, first by 2 for the minutes and then by 3 for the degrees & add to the place on the first, as for May 13th, a difference of 12 days (13 - 1):

Lilith May 1st .... 10:07 Taurus
12 days x 2-m, then x 3-d 36:24
(46:31 - 30:00 Taurus) .... 16:31 Gemini

Lilith's position before 1860

As stated on the preceding page Lilith has a minor cycle of 63 years which doubled gives 126 years as her major cycle, each reaching the same position. Compare her position Jan. 1, 1870 and Jan. 1, 1933 using her 63 year cycle, or for Jan. 1, 1996 using her 126 year cycle, all reaching 23:43 Capricorn.

To find her position before 1860, where her ephemeris begins on page 29 herein, say for the Declaration of Independence July 4th, 1776, use the 126 year cycle; always ADD since we are going forward.

```
                    1776
                  + 126 years
Lilith July 1st   1902 & 1776 ..... 13:40 Leo
Desired "  4th = 3 days x 3°2' =     9:06
Lilith July 4th, 1776 ........... 22:46 Leo
```

For this (23 Leo) Kozminsky gives "A rouser of men .....who will bring light and benefit to mankind."

To find her position still earlier in history, say for the final landing of Lief Ericcson, Oct. 18th, 1001 N.S., we multiply the 126 year cycle as often as necessary...in this case, 7 times or 882 years.

```
                    1001
                  + 882 years
Lilith Oct. 1st   1883 & 1001 .....  8:11 Pi.
Desired "  18th = 17 days x 3°2'   51:34 -"
Lilith Oct 18th, 1001 ........... 29:45 Ar.
```

For this (30 Aries) Kozminsky gives "Apt to enter into great schemes with very little backing, without regard for consequences."

Introducing Lilith

Lilith's "back" ground or back-street sphere of action is more easily recognized if we investigate ancient Hebraic literature. The Talmud tells us that she is the Queen of Evil and mother of demons and that she preceded Eve in Adam's life and was a degrading and destructive force - whereas Eve, the mother of human beings, is uplifting, moral & constructive. Thus Adam sponsored into the world the evil forces in man as well as the good residing as a possibility in each of us. Although born innocent, we are yet stained with "original sin" that is visited upon us by inheritance from Adam & Lilith. It is in this light that we introduce Lilith as the demoniac mother of demoniac beings on earth who may be only the tools of wrath chosen to carry out dire prophecies made before they were born.

The Bible is Hebraic, therefore the work of the prophets who were astrologers, and it has esoteric meaning (that is, confidential and directed to the select few who understand the occult or the secret doctrine, or are illuminated by divine inspiration and in-tuition). To understand the esoteric meaning involving Lilith and Eve we must recognize the allegorical handling of the subject in the Book of Genesis, and specifically the second chapter.

There, Eve also is personified as a satellite, a new moon emerging crescent and rib-shaped from the side of Adam, as the New Moon emerges from the side of the Sun. She is symbolic of man's better side, to increase & develop a better-than-demoniac strain, and in time outgrow or overcome the forces of evil inherent from Lilith. The overcoming must always be more against inner man than outer.

It was the famed astrologer Sepharial who named the dark moon Lilith, being versed in Hebraic literature wherein Lilith is also called Lilah. He recognized her nature in charts as being the same as that of Samson's De-lilah, the temptress who is man's betrayer because of his willing weakness.

It is twice written that IT IS NOT GOOD FOR MAN TO BE ALONE (Genesis) and NO MAN IS SAFE WHO IS IN A HOUSE ALONE (the Talmud); and also the witticism attributed to Mark Twain, "I can resist anything - except temptation". These are all darkly suggestive of the power of Lilith to ambush the unwary or weak, especially if she afflicts the rising degree or the planet ruling the rising Sign in the chart.

HISTORY may be hyphenated to his-story and thus Adam may have preferred to blame his downfall on the apple he shared with Eve - a weakness he could admit - rather than the forbidden fruit he shared with Lilith, which was a greater weakness he could not admit, knowing as he did that Lilith was evil.

In the Talmud, Lilith quarreled with Adam, left him and was pursued and overtaken by three angels. They sought unsuccessfully to persuade her toward a regenerate self but she refused in anger. Later, her insane jealousy of Adam's new companion Eve caused her to return in revenge and ensnare their children, and we blame her for Cain's fury against his brother Abel. There are people in many parts of the world today who employ amulets representing the three angels as charms to save themselves from the evil, ambushing and murderous power of Lilith.

The name Lilith in Hebrew means "night" and she is referred to in the Bible (Isaiah 34:14 Masoretic text) as the night hag and screech owl - and in the Septuagint as the vampire & night monster with special and evil power over childbirth, especially occurring at night, bent on injuring or destroying infants and their mothers within seven days after childbirth. Thus, Lilith in the natal 10th House which rules the mother, afflicted by bad aspect to a malefic planet (and more certainly when conjunct Caput Algol in 24 Taurus) is one indication of the death of the mother in childbirth. Lilith in the 5th House (the death-8th for the mother-10th) when the Moon or ruler of the 10th cusp is afflicted at birth is another indication of such misfortune.

The student should refer to the Universal Jewish Encyclopaedia under "Lilith" and may also find interesting the poem "Lilith" by George Sterling.

Nearly 6000 years have passed since the days of Lilith and Adam, and it is probable that her power in the natal chart has lost much ground. We find her still active, however, and it is well to study her natal and progressed position in the horoscope if only to know where and when to be on our guard. She is said to be exalted in Gemini (and therefore in her fall in Sagittarius) though no Sign dignity is allotted to her, but by House the 12th-of-ambush & self-undoing is a likely natural habitat for her.

Keywords for Lilith

Lilith is always SINISTER and MALEVOLENT in her intent and ultimate effect so that the matters and people represented by the house she is in will not be granted full measure of the good that otherwise could develop in the native's life in that department. She is DENYING, FRUSTRATING & CATASTROPHIC, bringing CHAOS to the affairs ruled by that house.

Under certain conditions, Lilith's keywords may be associated with the "bad" side of Neptune's and may also be those of the unfortunate attributes of the 12th House, having to do with SELF-UNDOING and MISTAKES or CRIMES committed deliberately. These keywords may be applied with caution to the person ruled by the house Lilith is in, because he is not necessarily evil in himself; Lilith is. We would say that he makes bad mistakes with his eyes open.

Lilith rules TEMPTATION, SEDUCTION and BETRAYAL that dishonor, if sufficiently afflictive. There is SUSCEPTIBILITY to strange influences, delusions and fatal fascinations, infatuation & COMPULSIONS. Under extreme affliction she is DEMORALIZING & debasing, ABNORMAL, illicit and ungodly, though such a person is not entirely responsible because under overwhelming compulsion that takes him off guard.

Lilith rules POISONING, ABORTION & STILLBIRTHS, death in childbirth, abnormal physical or emotional development, illness contrary to nature and inability to diagnose it correctly - until too late.

Lilith in the Chart

Lilith in the Chart

Because Lilith remains in the mysterious shadow to beckon and beguile those off guard, like a true Lorelei, she has an irresistible fascination for a great many of us, and particularly those with Mercury in an angular house (1st, 10th, 7th and 4th), because he represents curiosity and is active when angular; susceptible to attraction and to anything signalling, beckoning or mysterious. Her position should be noted in horary and mundane charts also.

Lilith in the Natal Chart

In the birth chart her effect is lifelong & may be related mainly to DENIAL involving the house in which she appears; this will be activated whenever she receives the conjunction of a major progressed planet or a strong transit, especially an eclipse. When Lilith herself progresses to conjunct a natal planet or angular cusp she denies security for the time being and upsets the status quo there, & this continues for the period of her orb (see page 21).

The more prominent or angular the natal Lilith, the more other people find the native FASCINATING, and to the opposite sex FRIENDLY and FLIRTATIOUS - even though unintentional. If afflicted at birth this is more pronounced and sure to cause jealousy or trouble in marriage. Warning means nothing because the trait is inborn and spontaneous, and may even make the native wonder at himself (or herself as the case may be). On the other hand, when Lilith is not prominent in the chart or is intercepted, no amount of instruction will teach the native how to be fascinating, or win friends, etc. Those in public life who are sedate & demure do not have Lilith prominent, so their audiences do not expect any "follow-me-lads-I'm-single" delightful manner.

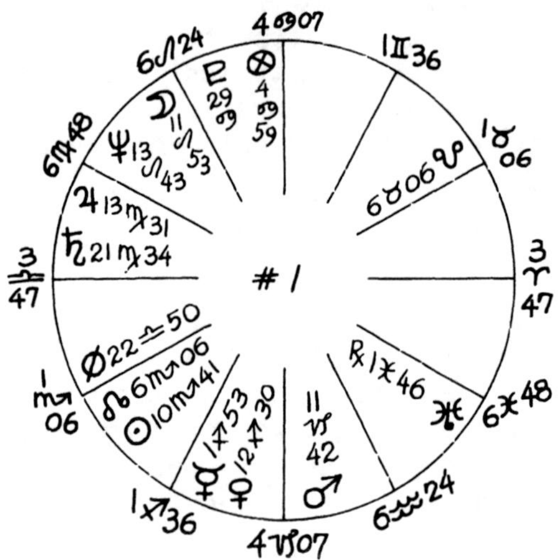

3:28:19 a.m. LMT Nov. 3, 1920, 33N54 94W59

This is the natal chart of a dwarf 4'3½", 110 lbs; born at full term, normal gestation period; one of five children, the others all normal in every way. Unmarried; strong, healthy and has extraordinarily muscular forearms. He is a favorite with all and makes friends easily (Lilith angular); is accepted socially by employer & has a good job as manager & actual cleanup-man for service-station restrooms.

Lilith in the Houses

Fundamentally, Lilith goes after human beings & is intent on injuring them PERSONALLY - which will be physically, materially or functionally according to whether she is in an angular, succeedent or cadent house in the natal chart. By and large, we group the houses in sets of four this way, and all of them employ as their first keyword that of the angular-1st, succeedent-2nd or cadent-3rd house in the First Quadrant of the wheel & always personal.

The 1st, 4th, 7th & 10th Houses are angular and DENY greatest good if Lilith is there. It will be physical (1st) or because of the family and father (4th), the partner or enemy (7th), or the employer or mother (10th), because all of these can afflict the native personally, being in evil aspect to the First House by conjunction, square or opposition. These are mundane aspects (formed by houses only), but if Lilith is in bad aspect to a malefic (or if she is conjunct an evil fixed star) she injures by zodiacal aspect also, both denying AND afflicting.

In the chart on the opposite page we see Lilith in the 1st House denying personal & physical good, and injuring the body by afflictive evil aspect to malefic Pluto - therefore the person is physically afflicted (a dwarf) which is a 1st House effect; & the malefic being in the 10th emphasizes the denial of vocation he would prefer; the 7th may refuse matrimony; the 4th (Mars there) denies home life & so he was rejected at birth & put out of the home.

SUBSTANCE (finances & possessions) is the keyword for the Second House which leads the succeedent group - therefore the Fifth, Eighth & Eleventh take that keyword as their first. In any of these succeedent houses, Lilith afflicts MATERIAL interests by conjunction, square and opposition to the 2nd House itself. It affects own substance (2nd), joint holdings or community property (5th, the 2nd for the family-4th), income by partnership, marriage, settlement or legacy (8th) & wages (the 11th, which is the income-2nd for the employment-10th).

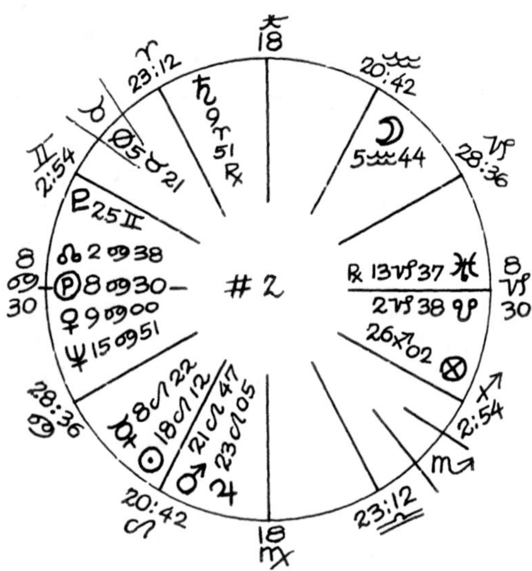

1:58:00 a.m. LMT Aug. 11, 1908 - 90W12 38N48

Because of serious brain injury in an accident, this man is unable to work for an employer so that he earns no actual wages (Lilith in 11th square to his ruler Moon and to a planet in his income-2nd).

The cadent houses include the 6th-of-functioning so that Lilith in any cadent house is MALFUNCTION. The native does what he chooses second because he cannot do what he chooses first. Lilith's POISONING is actual when she or her Solstice Point (page 22) is in the nutriment-6th. Involved with relatives, teachers, sickness, bondage, incarceration, trouble with children or they are unfortunate, and mistakes that lead to self-undoing & evil "karma".

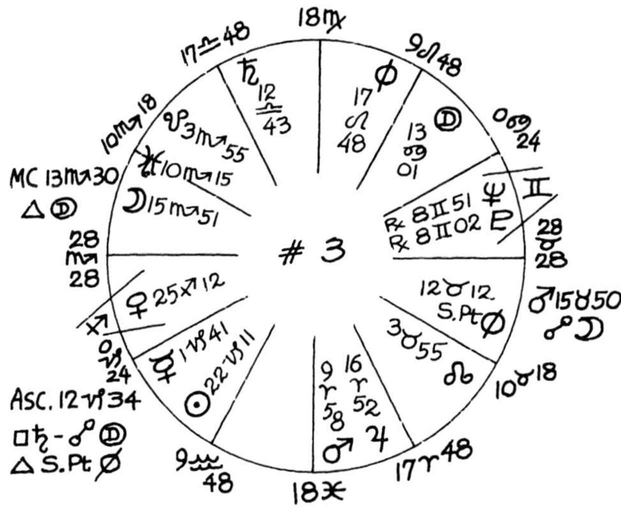

3:48:20 a.m. LMT Jan. 12, 1893 - 12E06 47N

This is the Nazi Hermann Goering's chart, equipped at birth for suicide by Lilith cadent & square the Moon-ruler-8th in the death Sign & suicide-Pisces decanate in the suicide 12th House. On the eve of his execution he committed suicide by poison (the Solstice Point in the 6th): note the progressions.

Lilith Intercepted

Lilith is a force to reckon with, and no chart can escape her presence - so that no one can count himself entirely invulnerable to her hostile power or think himself forever free of it. When Lilith is intercepted, however, she is HELD BACK & within bounds by the intercepting bars, and her influence is POSTPONED temporarily --- but only temporarily.

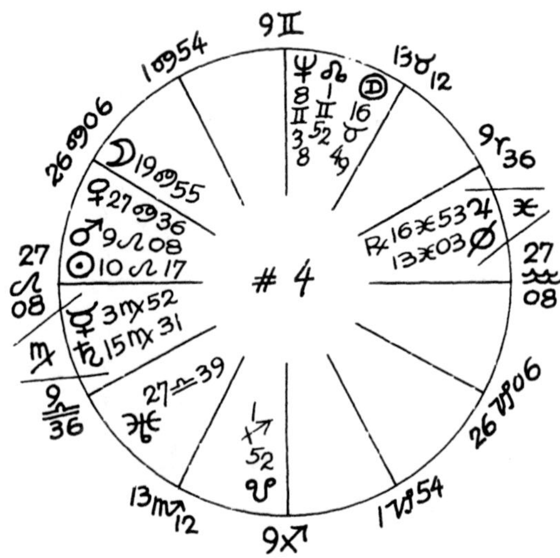

7:43:52 a.m. LMT Aug. 3, 1891 - 141E28 32S

Mars-ruler-death-8th in the murder-12th could have killed this man by age 2½ when progressed conjunct the Sun-ruler-Ascendant, but Lilith is intercepted so the native's death in battle (a form of murder) occurred in 1917 (arc 26:00) when directed Part of Death 13 Gemini (p. 22) squared Lilith in war-7th.

Lilith in the Pre-Natal Chart

When a severe physical affliction develops during the native's lifetime it must be accounted-for as a probability in his natal chart, and activated by major progressions later. But if it is a congenital (existing at birth) physical abnormality it developed before birth and will be shown in one of the charts covering the months of the pre-natal period. These mark the development or mal-development of the unborn child, and also designate the month during pregnancy when Lilith causes trouble.

The natal Moon always gives the first clue, so we will take the chart on page 10 for a dwarf, and note that the Moon conjuncts abnormal Neptune, who lames, stunts and deforms. The rules of Pre-Natal Astrology teach that the Moon's place at birth was the ascendant for all the charts for the gestation period, so that they all had 11:53 Leo rising with slow-moving Neptune always there to affect growth.

The Chart at Conception

The ascendant at birth is the place of the Moon at conception. For this birth Nov. 3, 1920, we go back nine months to find the Moon at 3:47 Libra in this case, and we note that conception occurred on Feb. 7, 1920. We set the chart for conception for that date, 11:53 Leo rising & the Moon 3:47 Libra, as presented on the next page herein (with malefic Neptune conjunct the ascendant as we anticipated).

5:03:35 p.m. LMT Feb. 7, 1920, 94W59 34N

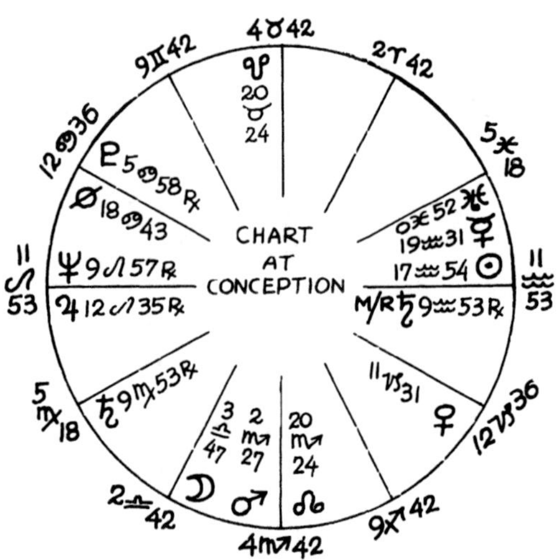

By mutual reception with Mercury, Saturn may be read also as back in his Sign Aquarius shown here, afflicting Neptune almost to the minute. He rules bone-development and regulates the height of the skeleton: when retrograde he withholds & shortens, shown also by natal Saturn square Venus-ruler-1st.

Here we see the enemy of both mother and child, Lilith, in the conception-Sign Cancer & afflicting Venus in Saturn's Sign Capricorn which governs the bone-cells, the building-blocks for the body - and thus the body is deformed in accordance with the deformity of the skeleton, ruled by Saturn himself.

Each time the Moon returns to approximately the same place as at conception we have a chart called a Pre-Natal Return with the same cusps as at conception, but the Sun and planets in new positions. The 1st Return on March 5th was without incident, but not the 2nd, at 1:26:17 p.m. LMT April 2nd as:

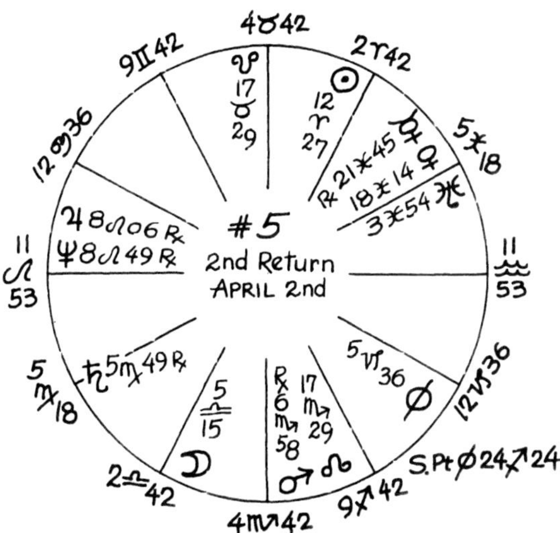

Because the 2nd Return immediately precedes the month of the "quickening" (manifestation of life), it is extremely sensitive to lunar affliction from Lilith. Lilith here exactly squares the Moon from Saturn's Sign, to develop dwarfism at this Return.

The co-operation of astrologer Katherine B. Tuttle in confirming these figures is greatly appreciated.

Lilith in the Horary Chart

In horary charts, Lilith discloses where danger of BETRAYAL or DENIAL threatens the one asking the question if in bad aspect to the Ascendant or its ruler as in Chart #6. In the 1st House afflicting its ruler, the querent often "gives himself away".

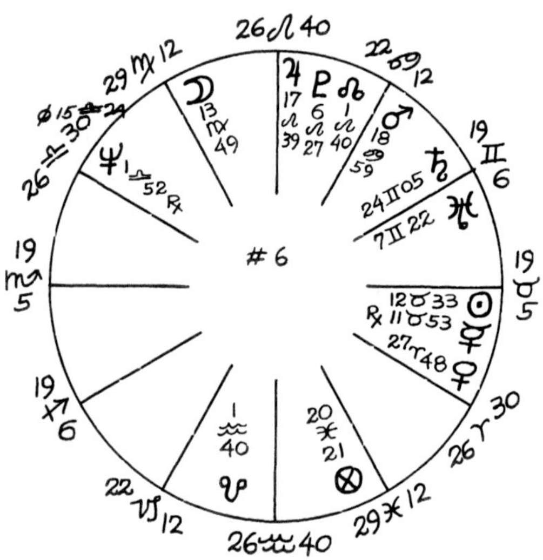

8:05 p.m. PDST May 2d, 1944 - 118W15 34N03

A friendly witness to the querent's traffic accident promised to testify for her in a suit for doctor bills but at the last moment refused to do so, denying the querent who then abandoned the matter. Her ruler Mars squared by Lilith in friendly-11th.

Lilith in the Mundane Chart

In mundane charts Lilith discloses where danger of BETRAYAL or DENIAL threatens the country or the government, business firms, etc., according to the house she is in and the house ruled by the planet she afflicts. In the 10th, disgrace of officials; the 5th affects the stock market & birth rate; the 7th, entanglements in war or the courts - with the public being deceived; in the 8th, the death rate; the 4th, the homeland, mining & real estate, etc.

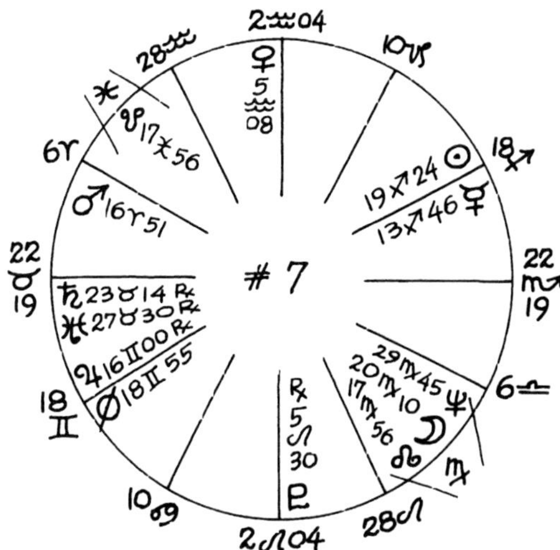

U.S.A. declares War on Germany Dec. 11, 1941

Lilith conjuncts the substance-2nd and opposes the Sun-ruler-homeland-4th in the death-rate 8th, with great loss in national resources and armed forces.

Lilith by Progression

Lilith may progress to aspect planets and cusps in the natal chart; may conjunct midpoints between planets, or may conjunct a planet's solstice point (see p. 22). Allow an orb of 1 degree applying & 1 degree separating for waxing and waning effects. Conjunctions and squares are the strongest aspects and the conjunction tempts the native to unwise or rash action that is generally emotional in nature, while the square involves a loss as illustrated by Chart #4 on page 14 whose Lilith we will progress.

Lilith's daily motion of 3-dg 2-min is taken as her yearly motion in finding her progressed place. If the degrees then exceed 30 or 60, etc. subtract the Sign she is in and as many more as necessary.

Lilith in the chart on p. 14 ..	13:03	Pisces
Age 12 (12 x 2, then x 3)	36:24	
(1 Sign too many)	49:27	
Subtract the Sign she is in ...	30:00	Pisces
Progressed Lilith, age 12	19:27	Aries

At age 12, when this native's progressed Lilith in 19 Aries exactly squared natal Moon, his mother died in childbirth, the infant also. For confirmation, note that the age-arc 12:00 moved Mercury-ruler-mother-10th exactly conjunct Saturn ruler of her death-8th - & Venus co-significator of mothers in 9 Leo conjoined Mars ruler death-in-his-circle.

Lilith's Solstice Point

The Solstice Point of Lilith (or any planet) is its distance from O-Cancer or O-Capricorn (whichever is nearer) carried across to the other side of the one used. Lilith's Solstice Point times the less-fortunate TURNING POINTS in the native's life when in aspect, and is easy to find: her REMAINING degrees in the Sign she is in are the degrees for her Solstice Point, and the Sign to use is the one on the same line with hers in this diagram:

Capricorn	:	Sagittarius
Aquarius	:	Scorpio
Pisces	:	Libra
Aries	:	Virgo
Taurus	:	Leo
Gemini	:	Cancer

Lilith in 13:03 degrees in the chart on page 14 has 16:57 remaining: she is in Pisces and the Sign on that line is Libra: 16:57 Libra is her Solstice Point therefore. Besides receiving aspects it also makes aspects by adding the age arc, marking turning points in the life. Thus, the native enlisted in World War I in 1914 at age arc 23:00. Added to Lilith's S. Pt 16:57 Libra gave 9:57 Scorpio which exactly squared Mars the warrior planet describing an unfortunate turning point (square) eventuating in his violent death in action three years later.

The Parts of Death and Peril

The 1st + the 8th - the Moon = (D) Part of Death.
The 1st + ruler 8th - Saturn = (P) Part of Peril.

Lilith in the Ingress Chart

By ingress is meant "to enter" and the four Ingress Charts each year are set for the Sun's entry into each of the 4 Cardinal Signs Aries, Cancer, Libra and Capricorn. They are of particular value in universal affairs since the cardinal Signs signify the cardinal points North, East, West & South thereby encompassing every part of the world. Note that the directions in that order bring us NEWS, & that is what the Ingress Charts always foretell.

For WORLD affairs in general and England's in particular, take the Ingress Chart set for London. For NATIONAL or LOCAL affairs elsewhere, we adjust that London chart to the longitude and latitude of the nation or city under consideration. (This is fully explained on p. 82 of "The Foundation of the Astrological Chart" by this writer.) Each ingress chart lasts three months & is immediately followed by the next one so that even he who runs may read the current trend for nations, cities and people.

Always show Lilith's position in the chart, and also her Solstice Point (see page 22) and remember that if either of these should contact the cusp of the 10th House or its ruler, then the locality or its governing head will be singled out for special attention during the ensuing three months. Do not give snap judgment, however, but always have three or four additional indications to support whatever you say. The first is always only a threat; it is the dire aspects in addition that confirm trouble.

In this Ingress Chart for the United States and therefore set for Washington, D. C. we find Lilith in 28:30 Gemini not afflicting anything: it is her Solstice Point in 1:30 Cancer that is important as a threat because it is only 46 minutes from exact conjunction to the Moon, ruling the 10th House and denoting DENIAL because that is one major keyword. If it were conjunct the 10th CUSP the denial would most afflict the country by possible BETRAYAL, but conjunct the RULER of the 10th, the representative of the nation, the President, we see the threat is against him personally, and it will eventuate during the ensuing three-month period of the ingress.

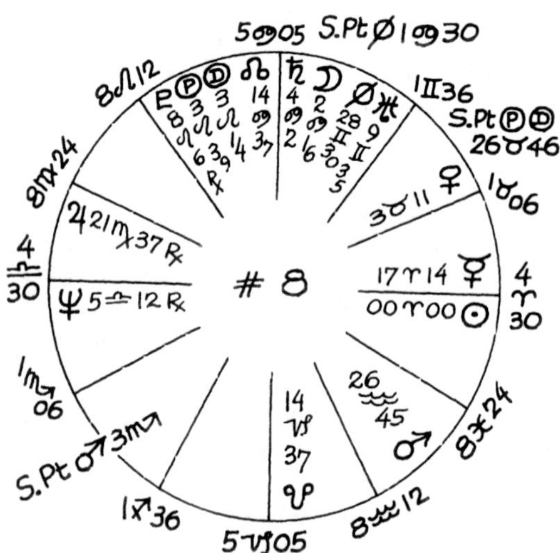

To support the threat revealed by Lilith's Solstice Point conjunct the President's ruler Moon we find that she is conjunct one malefic, Saturn, and square another, Neptune, besides being besieged or hemmed-in between the evil forces Uranus & Saturn, and not able to escape because there is no mutual reception (two planets in each other's Sign, which enables them to get out of trouble they get into).

When we find the affliction to the ruler of the 10th involves the ruler of the 5th or a malefic in the 5th (injury or death of the 10th House person) as the Moon conjunct Saturn does here, we work the Part of Peril (Ascendant plus the ruler of the 8th and then minus Saturn) which is (P) 3:39 Leo here. It squares the ruler of the 8th in the 8th, Venus, threatening serious danger that could mean death. We thus work the Part of Death (Ascendant plus the 8th and then minus the Moon) which is (D) 3:14 Leo here, exactly conjunct the Part of Peril & sharing its square to Venus, giving great cause for alarm. It is doubly apparent that the President may die.

It is the Solstice Point (D) 26:46 Taurus that exactly squares malefic Mars in the President's house of death that tells us he is to pass away in the ensuing three months of the ingress but it was the initial conjunction of Lilith's Solstice Point to his ruler Moon that led us to calculate (P) and (D) and thus make an accurate forecast for him.

This is the Aries Ingress Chart for Washington, 77-W, 39-N, at 6:29:44 p.m. LMT on March 20, 1945. Our President was Franklin Delano Roosevelt and he died suddenly (Moon-ruler-10th parallel Uranus) on April 12, 1945 the day of the New Moon in 22 Aries that semisquared Uranus-ruler-his-8th. Note that it occurred within a month of the ingress date. Wise astrologers who see this in advance will keep their own counsel & confide in only a trusted few.

* * * * *

EPHEMERIS for LILITH

Given for the first of each month
Always direct at 3-dg 2-min per day

Year	Jan	Feb	Mar	Apr	May	June
1860	6Gem16	10Vir31	5Sag40	9 Pi 55	10Gem25	13Vir22
1861	28Gem34	2Lib51	1Cap03	5Ari19	5Can22	8Lib18
1862	23Can56	28Lib12	23Cap24	27Ari18	27Can17	00Sco13
1863	16Leo19	20Sco35	15Aqu40	19Tau09	19Leo10	22Sco08
1864	8Vir38	12Sag48	7 Pi 53	11Gem00	10Vir59	14Sag04
1865	00Lib51	4Cap57	2Ari40	5Can47	5Lib54	9Cap05
1866	28Lib02	00Aqu03	24Ari25	27Can39	27Lib52	1Aqu09
1867	18Sco04	21Aqu53	16Tau13	19Leo35	19Sco56	23Aqu17
1868	10Sag02	13 Pi 39	8Gem06	11Vir33	12Sag02	15 Pi 31
1869	1Cap52	5Ari29	3Can04	6Lib41	7Cap17	10Ari42

Year	July	Aug	Sept	Oct	Nov	Dec
1860	12Sag19	16 Pi 16	19Gem13	19Vir09	23Sag05	24 Pi 18
1861	8Cap15	11Ari11	14Can07	14Lib12	18Cap27	19Ari40
1862	00Aqu11	3Tau08	6Leo06	6Sco38	10Aqu52	12Tau05
1863	22Aqu09	25Tau08	28Leo09	29Sco04	3 Pi 16	4Gem27
1864	14 Pi 08	17Gem12	20Vir29	21Sag34	25 Pi 40	26Gem45
1865	9Ari12	12Can21	16Lib00	17Cap01	21Ari02	22Can00
1866	1Tau22	4Leo37	8Sco30	9Aqu21	13Tau16	14Leo10
1867	23Tau38	27Leo07	00Sag55	1 Pi 45	5Gem29	6Vir15
1868	16Gem00	19Vir35	23Sag15	23 Pi 53	27Gem33	28Vir12
1869	11Can28	15Lib00	18Cap32	19Ari02	22Can36	23Lib06

Year	Jan	Feb	Mar	Apr	May	June
1870	26Cap43	00Tau30	25Can12	29Lib00	29Cap45	3Tau32
1871	18Aqu51	22Tau42	17Leo29	21Sco20	22Aqu10	26Tau01
1872	10 Pi 51	14Gem47	12Vir43	16Sag39	17 Pi 35	21Gem28
1873	5Ari57	10Can01	5Lib00	9Cap04	10Ari07	13Can41
1874	28Ari09	2Leo18	27Lib21	1Aqu30	2Tau37	5Leo48
1875	20Tau25	24Leo38	19Sco45	23Aqu58	24Tau53	27Leo51
1876	12Gem45	17Vir00	15Sag11	19 Pi 26	19Gem52	22Vir48
1877	8Can10	12Lib26	7Cap36	11Ari52	11Can48	14Lib44
1878	00Leo27	4Sco42	29Cap52	3Tau44	3Leo42	6Sco40
1879	22Leo49	27Sco02	22Aqu10	25Tau35	25Leo35	28Sco35

Year	July	Aug	Sept	Oct	Nov	Dec
1870	4Leo07	7Sco31	10Aqu56	11Tau21	14Leo46	15Sco11
1871	26Leo26	29Sco43	3 Pi 41	3Gem19	6Vir37	6Sag55
1872	21Vir39	24Sag50	28 Pi 01	28Gem12	1Lib33	1Cap54
1873	13Lib47	16Cap53	19Ari59	20Can05	23Lib11	24Cap00
1874	5Sco49	8Aqu51	11Tau52	11Leo54	15Sco01	16Aqu12
1875	27Sco49	00 Pi 47	3Gem45	3Vir43	7Sag17	8 Pi 30
1876	22Sag45	25 Pi 42	28Gem39	28Vir35	2Cap40	3Ari54
1877	14Cap40	18Ari36	21Can32	20Lib43	24Cap58	26Ari11
1878	6Aqu37	9Tau39	11Leo32	13Sco11	17Aqu24	18Tau35
1879	28Aqu35	1Gem35	4Vir35	5Sag39	9 Pi 50	10Gem58

Year	Jan	Feb	Mar	Apr	May	June
1880	15Vir09	19Sag19	17 Pi 20	20Gem24	20Vir28	23Sag31
1881	10Lib24	14Cap30	9Ari04	17Can13	12Lib22	15Cap31
1882	2Sco31	6Aqu31	00Tau52	4Leo07	4Sco22	7Aqu37
1883	24Sco29	28Aqu18	22Tau30	25Leo52	26Sco14	29Aqu36
1884	16Sag26	19 Pi 59	17Gem27	20Vir58	21Sag28	24 Pi 59
1885	11Cap19	14Ari57	9Can32	13Lib10	13Cap46	17Ari24
1886	3Aqu07	6Tau52	1Leo34	5Sco19	6Aqu03	9Tau48
1887	25Aqu15	29Tau05	23Leo48	27Sco38	28Aqu28	2Gem30
1888	17 Pi 03	21Gem05	19Vir02	23Sag04	24 Pi 03	27Gem43
1889	12Ari12	16Can18	11Lib17	15Cap22	16Ari25	19Can56

Year	July	Aug	Sept	Oct	Nov	Dec
1880	23 Pi 35	26Gem39	00Lib04	1Cap08	5Ari14	6Can18
1881	15Ari40	18Can49	22Lib35	23Cap33	27Ari33	28Can31
1882	7Tau52	11Leo09	15Sco01	15Aqu53	19Tau45	20Leo37
1883	29Tau58	3Vir41	7Sag26	8 Pi 11	11Gem56	12Vir41
1884	25Gem30	29Vir09	2Cap47	3Ari24	7Can02	7Lib39
1885	17Can58	21Lib29	25Cap00	25Ari30	29Can01	29Lib31
1886	10Leo33	13Sco54	17Aqu15	17Tau36	20Leo57	21Sco18
1887	2Vir42	5Sag57	9 Pi 13	9Gem28	12Vir43	13Sag03
1888	27Vir53	1Cap02	4Ari12	4Can21	7Lib31	8Cap07
1889	19Lib59	23Cap04	25Ari08	26Can12	29Lib17	00Aqu16

Year	Jan	Feb	Mar	Apr	May	June
1890	4Tau26	8Leo36	3Sco40	7Aqu50	8Tau58	12Leo00
1891	26Tau41	00Vir55	26Sco03	00 Pi 16	1Gem04	4Vir02
1892	19Gem08	23Vir24	21Sag35	25 Pi 50	26Gem03	28Vir59
1893	14Can26	18Lib42	13Cap52	18Ari02	17Can59	20Lib55
1894	6Leo51	11Sco04	6Aqu11	9Tau52	9Leo50	12Sco48
1895	29Leo07	3Sag20	28Aqu27	1Gem42	1Vir44	4Sag45
1896	21Vir24	25Sag33	23 Pi 26	26Gem32	26Vir37	29Sag43
1897	16Lib38	20Cap43	15Ari10	18Can21	18Lib31	21Cap42
1898	8Sco44	12Aqu42	6Tau59	10Leo16	10Sco33	13Aqu50
1899	00Sag46	4 Pi 26	28Tau50	2Vir14	2Sag38	6 Pi 02

Year	July	Aug	Sept	Oct	Nov	Dec
1890	12Sco00	15Aqu01	18Tau02	18Leo02	21Sco16	22Aqu28
1891	4Sag00	6 Pi 58	9Gem55	9Vir53	13Sag39	14 Pi 52
1892	28Sag55	1Ari51	4Can47	4Lib44	8Cap56	10Ari10
1893	20Cap53	23Ari49	26Can45	27Lib12	1Aqu26	2Tau38
1894	12Aqu47	15Tau45	18Leo44	19Sco30	23Aqu43	24Tau54
1895	4 Pi 46	7Gem47	10Vir50	11Sag57	16 Pi 07	17Gem14
1896	29 Pi 48	2Can54	6Lib24	7Cap26	11Ari31	12Can33
1897	21Ari52	25Can03	28Lib54	29Cap50	3Tau49	4Leo45
1898	14Tau07	17Leo30	21Sco22	22Aqu12	26Tau04	26Leo54
1899	6Gem26	10Vir00	13Sag45	14 Pi 28	18Gem13	18Vir56

Year	Jan	Feb	Mar	Apr	May	June
1900	22Sag41	26 Pi 13	20Gem42	24Vir14	24Sag45	28 Pi 16
1901	14Cap25	18Ari05	12Can42	16Lib22	17Cap01	20Ari41
1902	6Aqu16	10Tau03	4Leo52	8Sco39	9Aqu26	13Tau13
1903	28Aqu13	2Gem07	27Leo03	00Sag57	1 Pi 51	5Gem45
1904	20 Pi 13	24Gem14	22Vir12	26Sag14	27 Pi 14	00Can59
1905	15Ari24	19Can31	14Lib34	18Cap41	19Ari46	23Can09
1906	7Tau39	11Leo50	6Sco55	11Aqu06	12Tau13	15Leo12
1907	29Tau55	4Vir09	29Sco17	3 Pi 31	4Gem15	7Vir12
1908	22Gem16	26Vir32	24Sag43	28 Pi 59	29Gem13	2Lib09
1909	17Can40	21Lib56	17Cap05	21Ari10	21Can07	24Lib04

Year	July	Aug	Sept	Oct	Nov	Dec
1900	28Gem47	2Lib26	6Cap02	6Ari37	10Can13	10Lib48
1901	21Can18	24Lib46	28Cap14	28Ari42	2Leo11	2Sco39
1902	13Leo40	17Sco00	20Aqu20	20Tau40	24Leo00	24Sco21
1903	5Vir57	9Sag11	12 Pi 35	12Gem38	15Vir51	16Sag12
1904	1Lib06	4Cap14	7Ari22	7Can29	10Lib37	11Cap17
1905	23Lib12	26Cap15	29Ari18	29Can21	2Sco24	3Aqu28
1906	15Sco12	18Aqu11	21Tau10	21Leo10	24Sco29	25Aqu41
1907	7Sag09	10 Pi 06	13Gem03	13Vir00	16Sag46	18 Pi 00
1908	2Cap05	5Ari01	7Can57	7Lib54	12Cap10	13Ari24
1909	24Cap01	26Ari58	29Can55	00Sco20	4Aqu35	5Tau48

Year	Jan	Feb	Mar	Apr	May	June
1910	10Leo03	14Sco18	9Aqu26	13Tau01	13Leo00	15Sco58
1911	2Vir21	6Sag33	1 Pi 39	4Gem50	4Vir52	7Sag54
1912	24Vir36	28Sag44	26 Pi 38	29Gem45	29Vir52	2Cap58
1913	19Lib50	23Cap53	18Ari20	21Can32	21Lib44	24Cap56
1914	11Sco55	15Aqu49	10Tau07	13Leo26	13Sco44	17Aqu03
1915	3Sag56	7 Pi 31	1Gem55	5Vir22	5Sag48	9 Pi 15
1916	25Sag42	29 Pi 20	26Gem52	00Lib27	1Cap00	4Ari35
1917	20Cap33	24Ari15	18Can54	22Lib36	23Cap17	26Ari59
1918	12Aqu23	16Tau13	10Leo58	14Sco48	15Aqu37	19Tau27
1919	4 Pi 23	8Gem18	3Vir14	7Sag09	8 Pi 04	12Gem00

Year	July	Aug	Sept	Oct	Nov	Dec
1910	15Aqu57	18Tau56	21Leo55	22Sco47	26Aqu59	28Tau09
1911	7 Pi 56	10Gem59	14Vir08	15Sag14	19 Pi 22	20Gem28
1912	3Ari04	6Can10	9Lib42	10Cap43	14Ari46	15Can47
1913	25Ari08	28Can20	2Sco11	3Aqu06	7Tau03	7Leo58
1914	17Tau21	20Leo48	24Sco38	25Aqu26	29Tau16	00Vir06
1915	9Gem41	13Vir19	17Sag00	17 Pi 40	21Gem21	22Vir01
1916	5Can08	8Lib43	12Cap17	12Ari50	16Can24	16Lib57
1917	27Can36	1Sco02	4Aqu28	4Tau54	8Leo20	8Sco46
1918	19Leo58	23Sco16	26Aqu34	26Tau52	00Vir10	00Sag28
1919	12Vir12	15Sag24	18 Pi 36	18Gem48	22Vir00	22Sag25

Year	Jan	Feb	Mar	Apr	May	June
1920	26 Pi 28	00Can31	28Vir31	2Cap34	3Ari35	7Can16
1921	21Ari40	25Can48	20Lib50	24Cap58	26Ari04	29Can22
1922	13Tau54	18Leo06	13Sco12	17Aqu24	18Tau25	21Leo23
1923	6Gem16	10Vir31	5Sag40	9 Pi 55	10Gem25	13Vir22
1924	28Gem34	2Lib51	1Cap03	5Ari19	5Can23	8Lib19
1925	23Can57	28Lib12	23Cap23	27Ari19	27Can16	00Sco13
1926	16Leo19	20Sco34	15Aqu41	19Tau09	19Leo09	22Sco09
1927	8Vir38	12Sag49	7 Pi 52	10Gem58	11Vir01	14Sag05
1928	00Lib51	4Cap57	2Ari39	5Can47	5Lib55	9Cap04
1929	26Lib02	00Aqu03	24Ari25	27Can39	27Lib53	1Aqu08

Year	July	Aug	Sept	Oct	Nov	Dec
1920	7Lib22	10Cap28	13Ari34	13Can40	16Lib46	17Cap32
1921	29Lib24	2Aqu26	5Tau28	5Leo30	8Sco32	9Aqu42
1922	21Sco21	24Aqu20	27Tau19	27Leo18	00Sag48	2 Pi 01
1923	12Sag19	16 Pi 16	19Gem13	19Vir10	23Sag04	24 Pi 18
1924	8Cap15	11Ari11	14Can07	14Lib12	18Cap27	19Ari41
1925	00Aqu11	3Tau08	6Leo06	6Sco38	10Aqu52	12Tau04
1926	22Aqu09	25Tau08	28Leo08	29Sco05	3 Pi 16	4Gem27
1927	14 Pi 08	17Gem12	20Vir29	21Sag34	25 Pi 40	26Gem45
1928	9Ari12	12Can21	16Lib00	17Cap01	21Ari01	22Can01
1929	1Tau22	4Leo37	8Sco29	9Aqu22	13Tau16	14Leo10

Year	Jan	Feb	Mar	Apr	May	June
1930	18Sco04	21Aqu53	16Tau13	19Leo35	19Sco56	23Aqu17
1931	10Sag02	13 Pi 39	8Gem05	11Vir34	12Sag02	15 Pi 31
1932	1Cap52	5Ari29	3Can04	6Lib41	7Cap17	10Ari53
1933	26Cap42	00Tau26	25Can06	28Lib50	29Cap33	3Tau17
1934	18Aqu35	22Tau27	17Leo14	21Sco06	21Aqu56	25Tau48
1935	10 Pi 36	14Gem32	9Vir26	13Sag22	14 Pi 18	18Gem11
1936	2Ari40	6Can44	4Lib45	8Cap49	9Ari50	13Can26
1937	28Ari09	2Leo18	27Lib21	1Aqu30	2Tau37	5Leo49
1938	20Tau25	24Leo38	19Sco45	23Aqu58	24Tau53	27Leo51
1939	12Gem45	17Vir00	15Sag11	19 Pi 26	19Gem52	22Vir48

Year	July	Aug	Sept	Oct	Nov	Dec
1930	23Tau38	27Leo07	00Sag55	1 Pi 45	5Gem29	6Vir15
1931	16Gem00	19Vir35	23Sag15	23 Pi 53	27Gem33	28Vir12
1932	11Can28	15Lib00	18Cap32	19Ari03	22Can35	23Lib06
1933	3Leo53	7Sco18	10Aqu43	11Tau06	14Leo31	14Sco54
1934	26Leo12	29Sco29	2 Pi 46	3Gem03	6Vir20	6Sag37
1935	18Vir22	21Sag33	24 Pi 44	24Gem55	28Vir16	28Sag37
1936	13Lib32	16Cap38	19Ari44	19Can50	22Lib56	23Cap45
1937	5Sco49	8Aqu51	11Tau52	11Leo54	15Sco01	16Aqu12
1938	27Sco49	00 Pi 47	3Gem45	3Vir43	7Sag17	8 Pi 30
1939	22Sag45	25 Pi 42	28Gem39	28Vir35	2Cap40	3Ari54

Year	Jan	Feb	Mar	Apr	May	June
1940	8Can10	12Lib25	7Cap36	11Ari52	11Can48	14Lib44
1941	00Leo27	4Sco42	29Cap52	3Tau44	3Leo42	6Sco40
1942	22Leo49	27Sco02	22Aqu10	25Tau35	25Leo36	28Sco35
1943	15Vir09	19Sag19	17 Pi 20	20Gem24	20Vir28	23Sag31
1944	10Lib24	19Cap30	9Ari04	12Can13	12Lib22	15Cap31
1945	2Sco31	6Aqu31	00Tau52	4Leo07	4Sco22	7Aqu38
1946	24Sco29	28Aqu18	22Tau30	25Leo52	26Sco14	29Aqu36
1947	16Sag27	19 Pi 59	17Gem27	20Vir58	21Sag28	24 Pi 58
1948	11Cap19	14Ari57	9Can31	13Lib10	13Cap46	17Ari24
1949	3Aqu07	6Tau52	1Leo34	5Sco19	6Aqu03	9Tau48

Year	July	Aug	Sept	Oct	Nov	Dec
1940	14Cap40	18Ari36	21Can32	20Lib43	24Cap58	26Ari11
1941	6Aqu37	9Tau34	12Leo32	13Sco00	17Aqu24	18Tau35
1942	28Aqu35	1Gem35	4Vir35	5Sag39	9 Pi 50	10Gem58
1943	23 Pi 35	26Gem40	1Lib04	1Cap08	5Ari14	6Can18
1944	15Ari40	18Can49	22Lib35	23Cap33	27Ari33	28Can31
1945	7Tau52	11Leo09	15Sco01	15Aqu53	19Tau45	20Leo38
1946	29Tau58	3Vir41	7Sag26	8 Pi 11	11Gem56	12Vir41
1947	25Gem30	29Vir09	2Cap47	3Ari24	7Can02	7Lib39
1948	17Can58	21Lib29	25Cap00	25Ari30	29Can02	29Lib31
1949	10Leo33	13Sco54	17Aqu15	17Tau36	20Leo57	21Sco18

Year	Jan	Feb	Mar	Apr	May	June
1950	25Aqu10	29Tau05	23Leo48	27Sco38	28Aqu28	2Gem30
1951	17 Pi 04	21Gem05	19Vir03	23Sag04	24 Pi 03	27Gem42
1952	12Ari12	16Can18	11Lib17	15Cap22	16Ari26	19Can55
1953	4Tau26	8Leo36	3Sco40	7Aqu50	8Tau58	12Leo00
1954	26Tau41	00Vir55	26Sco04	00 Pi 16	1Gem04	4Vir02
1955	19Gem08	23Vir24	21Sag35	25 Pi 50	26Gem03	28Vir59
1956	14Can26	18Lib42	13Cap52	18Ari02	17Can59	20Lib55
1957	6Leo51	11Sco04	6Aqu11	9Tau52	9Leo50	12Sco48
1958	29Leo07	3Sag20	28Aqu28	1Gem42	1Vir44	4Sag45
1959	21Vir24	25Sag33	23 Pi 26	26Gem32	26Vir37	29Sag43

Year	July	Aug	Sept	Oct	Nov	Dec
1950	2Vir42	5Sag57	9 Pi 12	9Gem28	12Vir43	13Sag03
1951	27Vir33	1Cap02	4Ari12	4Can21	7Lib31	8Cap07
1952	19Lib59	23Cap04	25Ari08	26Can12	29Lib17	00Aqu16
1953	12Sco00	15Aqu01	18Tau02	18Leo02	21Sco16	22Aqu28
1954	4Sag00	6 Pi 58	9Gem55	9Vir53	13Sag39	14 Pi 52
1955	28Sag55	1Ari51	4Can47	4Lib44	8Cap56	10Ari10
1956	20Cap53	23Ari49	26Can45	27Lib12	1Aqu27	2Tau38
1957	12Aqu47	15Tau45	18Leo44	19Sco30	23Aqu43	24Tau54
1958	4 Pi 46	7Gem47	10Vir50	11Sag57	16 Pi 07	17Gem13
1959	29 Pi 48	2Can54	6Lib24	7Cap26	11Ari31	12Can33

Year	Jan	Feb	Mar	Apr	May	June
1960	16Lib38	20Cap43	15Ari10	18Can21	18Lib31	21Cap42
1961	8Sco44	12Aqu42	6Tau59	10Leo16	10Sco33	13Aqu50
1962	00Sag46	4 Pi 26	28Tau50	2Vir14	2Sag38	6 Pi 02
1963	22Sag41	26 Pi 13	20Gem42	24Vir14	24Sag43	28 Pi 16
1964	14Cap25	18Ari04	12Can42	16Lib22	17Cap01	20Ari41
1965	6Aqu16	10Tau03	4Leo52	8Sco39	9Aqu26	13Tau13
1966	28Aqu13	2Gem07	27Leo03	00Sag57	1 Pi 51	5Gem45
1967	20 Pi 13	24Gem14	22Vir12	26Sag14	27 Pi 14	00Can59
1968	15Ari24	19Can31	14Lib34	18Cap41	19Ari46	23Can09
1969	7Tau38	11Leo50	6Sco55	11Aqu06	12Tau13	15Leo02

Year	July	Aug	Sept	Oct	Nov	Dec
1960	21Ari52	25Can03	28Lib54	29Cap50	3Tau49	4Leo45
1961	14Tau07	17Leo30	21Sco23	22Aqu12	26Tau04	26Leo34
1962	6Gem26	10Vir00	13Sag45	14 Pi 28	18Gem13	18Vir56
1963	28Gem47	2Lib26	6Cap02	6Ari57	10Can13	10Lib48
1964	21Can18	24Lib46	28Cap14	28Ari42	2Leo11	2Sco39
1965	13Leo40	17Sco00	20Aqu20	20Tau40	24Leo00	24Sco21
1966	5Vir57	9Sag11	12 Pi 35	12Gem38	15Vir51	16Sag12
1967	1Lib06	4Cap14	7Ari22	7Can28	10Lib37	11Cap17
1968	23Lib12	26Cap15	29Ari18	29Can21	2Sco24	3Aqu28
1969	15Sco12	18Aqu11	21Tau10	21Leo10	24Sco29	25Aqu41

Year	Jan	Feb	Mar	Apr	May	June
1970	29Tau55	4Vir09	29Sco17	3 Pi 31	4Gem15	7Vir12
1971	22Gem16	26Vir32	24Sag43	28 Pi 59	29Gem13	2Lib09
1972	17Can40	21Lib56	17Cap04	21Ari10	21Can07	24Lib05
1973	10Leo05	14Sco18	9Aqu26	13Tau01	13Leo00	15Sco57
1974	2Vir21	6Sag37	1 Pi 39	4Gem50	4Vir52	7Sag54
1975	24Vir36	28Sag44	26 Pi 38	29Gem45	29Vir53	2Cap58
1976	19Lib50	23Cap53	18Ari20	21Can32	21Lib44	24Cap56
1977	11Sco55	15Aqu48	10Tau08	13Leo26	13Sco44	17Aqu03
1978	5Sag56	7 Pi 31	1Gem54	5Vir23	5Sag48	9 Pi 15
1979	25Sag42	29 Pi 20	26Gem52	00Lib27	1Cap00	4Ari35

Year	July	Aug	Sept	Oct	Nov	Dec
1970	7Sag09	10 Pi 05	13Gem03	13Vir00	16Sag46	18 Pi 00
1971	2Cap05	5Ari01	7Can57	7Lib54	12Cap10	13Ari24
1972	24Cap01	26Ari58	29Can54	00Sco20	4Aqu35	5Tau48
1973	15Aqu57	18Tau56	21Leo55	22Sco47	26Aqu58	28Tau10
1974	7 Pi 56	10Gem59	14Vir08	15Sag14	19 Pi 22	20Gem28
1975	3Ari04	6Can10	9Lib41	10Cap43	14Ari47	15Can47
1976	25Ari08	28Can20	2Sco11	3Aqu06	7Tau03	7Leo58
1977	17Tau21	20Leo48	24Sco38	25Aqu26	29Tau16	00Vir06
1978	9Gem41	13Vir19	17Sag00	17 Pi 40	21Gem22	22Vir00
1979	5Can08	8Lib43	12Cap17	12Ari30	16Can24	16Lib57

Year	Jan	Feb	Mar	Apr	May	June
1980	20Cap33	24Ari15	18Can54	22Lib36	23Cap17	26Ari59
1981	12Aqu35	16Tau13	10Leo58	14Sco48	15Aqu37	19Tau28
1982	4 Pi 23	8Gem18	3Vir14	7Sag09	8 Pi 04	12Gem00
1983	26 Pi 28	00Can31	28Vir31	2Cap34	3Ari35	7Can16
1984	21Ari40	25Can48	20Lib50	24Cap58	26Ari05	29Can22
1985	13Tau54	18Leo06	13Sco12	17Aqu24	18Tau28	21Leo23
1986	6Gem16	10Vir31	5Sag40	9 Pi 55	10Gem25	13Vir22
1987	28Gem34	2Lib51	1Cap03	5Ari19	5Can23	8Lib19
1988	23Can57	28Lib12	23Cap23	27Ari19	27Can16	00Sco13
1989	16Leo19	20Sco34	15Aqu41	19Tau09	19Leo10	22Sco09

Year	July	Aug	Sept	Oct	Nov	Dec
1980	27Can36	1Sco03	4Aqu28	4Tau54	8Leo20	8Sco46
1981	19Leo58	23Sco16	26Aqu34	26Tau52	00Vir10	00Sag28
1982	12Vir12	15Sag24	18 Pi 36	18Gem48	20Vir00	22Sag25
1983	7Lib22	10Cap28	13Ari34	13Can40	16Lib46	17Cap32
1984	29Lib24	2Aqu26	5Tau28	5Leo30	8Sco32	9Aqu42
1985	21Sco21	24Aqu20	27Tau19	27Leo18	00Sag48	2 Pi 01
1986	12Sag19	16 Pi 16	19Gem13	19Vir10	25Sag04	24 Pi 18
1987	8Cap15	11Ari11	14Can07	14Lib12	18Cap27	19Ari41
1988	00Aqu11	3Tau08	6Leo06	6Sco38	10Aqu52	12Tau04
1989	22Aqu09	25Tau08	28Leo08	29Sco05	3 Pi 16	4Gem27

Year	Jan	Feb	Mar	Apr	May	June
1990	8Vir38	12Sag49	7 Pi 52	10Gem58	11Vir02	14Sag05
1991	00Lib51	4Cap57	2Ari39	5Can47	5Lib55	9Cap04
1992	26Lib02	00Aqu03	24Ari25	27Can39	27Lib53	1Aqu08
1993	18Sco04	21Aqu53	16Tau13	19Leo35	19Sco56	23Aqu17
1994	10Sag02	13 Pi 39	8Gem05	11Vir34	12Sag02	15 Pi 32
1995	1Cap52	5Ari29	3Can04	6Lib41	7Cap17	10Ari43
1996	26Cap42	00Tau25	25Can06	28Lib50	29Cap33	3Tau17
1997	18Aqu35	22Tau27	17Leo14	21Sco06	21Aqu56	25Tau48
1998	10 Pi 36	14Gem32	9Vir26	13Sag22	14 Pi 18	18Gem11
1999	2Ari40	6Can44	4Lib45	8Cap49	9Ari50	13Can26

Year	July	Aug	Sept	Oct	Nov	Dec
1990	14 Pi 08	17Gem12	20Vir29	21Sag34	25 Pi 40	26Gem45
1991	9Ari12	12Can21	16Lib00	17Cap01	21Ari01	22Can01
1992	1Tau22	4Leo37	8Sco29	9Aqu22	13Tau16	14Leo10
1993	23Tau38	27Leo07	00Sag55	1 Pi 44	5Gem30	6Vir15
1994	16Gem00	19Vir35	23Sag15	23 Pi 53	27Gem33	28Vir12
1995	11Can28	15Lib00	18Cap32	10Ari03	22Can35	23Lib06
1996	3Leo53	7Sco18	10Aqu43	11Tau06	14Leo31	14Sco54
1997	26Leo12	29Sco29	2 Pi 46	3Gem05	6Vir20	6Sag37
1998	18Vir22	21Sag33	24 Pi 44	24Gem55	28Vir16	28Sag37
1999	13Lib32	18Cap38	19Ari44	19Can50	22Lib56	23Cap45

* * * * *

CPSIA information can be obtained at www.ICGtesting.com
Printed in the USA
LVOW06s0301310815

452166LV00028B/716/P